# THE LIFE OF FAITH
## RECORDED HERE BELONGS TO:

_____

### THESE REFLECTIONS WERE RECORDED BETWEEN:

Start date: _____

Completion date: _____

THIS JOURNAL IS DEDICATED TO:

_____

_____

_____

_____

# CONTENTS

**00**  **BEFORE YOU BEGIN**  i
*Introduction to this journal*

**01**  **ABOUT ME**  1
*Who I am and where I came from*

**02**  **A VIEW FROM ABOVE**  11
*Favorites and foundations of my faith*

**03**  **BEGINNINGS OF FAITH**  33
*Early encounters with God*

**04**  **GROWING & QUESTIONING**  55
*The search for authentic faith*

## 05 LOVE & RELATIONSHIPS
*The bonds that shape faith* — 71

## 06 WORK & SERVICE
*Calling, purpose and serving others* — 89

## 07 THROUGH THE VALLEY
*God in pain, loss and uncertainty* — 103

## 08 MOUNTAINTOP MOMENTS
*Joy, blessings and answered prayers* — 117

## 09 EVERYDAY FAITH
*Faith in the ordinary rhythms of life* — 133

## 10 THE HARVEST
*Lessons, insights and gathered wisdom* — 145

| **11** | **THE HEART OF THANKS**<br>*Gratitude across a lifetime* | 163 |

| **12** | **THE OFFERING**<br>*What I leave in love and faith* | 177 |

| **13** | **EVERLASTING FAITH**<br>*The future and beyond this worldly life* | 199 |

| **B** | **A CLOSING BLESSING**<br>*For the journey lived and ahead* | 215 |

| **S** | **STORIES CONTINUED** | 221 |

| **P** | **LISTING OF PROMPTS** | 229 |

# BEFORE YOU BEGIN

There is a story behind every
life of faith.

Some stories are marked by
steady devotion, others by doubt,
renewal, or sudden awakening.

Each one carries its own wisdom
formed through hardship, love, trust,
prayer, and perseverance.

Every life has a story of
faith worth telling.

EVERY life of FAITH, *has a story.*

# A MESSAGE FROM CAIT

Many of us go to great lengths to record and share aspects of our lives. We catalogue photos, recipes, and favourite songs. We make lists of the places we've been, people we've met, and milestones we've reached. We keep these memories for ourselves and for others so they might remember who we were and what our lives contained.

Fewer of us, however, record the story of our life of faith—the larger arc of our relationship with God over our lifetime; the story behind all the other stories. Many of us keep to ourselves the critical moments of fear, doubt and discovery. Our most enduring prayers. Major blessings received. Or the insights and grace that steadied and strengthened us.

I came to reflect on this after my mother died, leaving this earthly realm. In that time, and since, I realized how little I knew of her faith. I had seen her faith lived out day by day, but did not know the details of how it evolved or its depths. I wish I had asked more, listened longer. Perhaps those conversations would have brought further comfort to her in her final years—and helped me now, as I continue here, on this path.

It was this reflection that inspired *A Life of Faith*. Within these pages are some of the things we spoke of, and some of the questions I never got to ask. They are offered to you, to answer for yourself—to trace how God has moved through your life.

What you write here will become a keepsake for those who you love and who loves you, and a testimony to the living faith that has shaped you. May these reflections also deepen your gratitude, strengthen your trust, and bear witness to the story of grace still unfolding.

*Wherever you find yourself* IN YOUR LIFE OF **FAITH,** you already have *stories to tell.*

## WHO THIS JOURNAL IS FOR

This journal is for anyone walking the path of faith and wishing to remember how God has been present along the way. You may be in the later years of life, looking back with gratitude; or in mid-life, pausing to take stock of how far grace has carried you; or even at the start of your life of faith, inspired and looking to understand how you even got to this point.

Ultimately, if you find yourself beyond your first encounter with God, there are questions here you can answer and pages here for you to fill. It's never too early or too late to start reflecting on your life that led to and forms your faith.

While this is a journal for one person, it can be enjoyable and nourishing to share the journaling experience. Consider sharing what you write in the coming pages with others close to you, or work through this book together, sharing entries as you go.

## WHAT YOU NEED TO START

All you need to start is this journal, a pen, time, a quiet space that supports deep reflection, and a willingness to open your mind and heart to your life and yourself—the thoughts, feelings, emotions, memories that will arise. This simplicity is at the heart of journaling, contemplation and reflection.

There is no right way to move through this journal. It is designed to be completed over days, months, or even years. So, take the approach that works for you in any moment – move through from beginning to end or go to what interests you. My hope is that you find yourself drawn to pick up this journal each week and respond to a number of the prompts, allowing reflection to become part of your daily life.

*Everything you have* experienced IS PART OF YOUR *story of* FAITH.

## A NOTE ON JOURNAL PROMPTS

You will find two kinds of prompts in this journal—questions (?) and statements to complete (…). They are used intentionally to elicit different kinds of responses. Over time, the voice of inquiry (question) becomes the voice of experience (statement). Notice if this makes a difference for you.

## WHEN A PROMPT DOESN'T FIT

Some prompts may not fit your life experience. Let that be part of your reflection. The wording of a prompt is not meant to limit your story or imply that anything is missing from it.

For example, perhaps God became part of your life during adulthood. Therefore, in response to questions of faith during early years of life, you might simply state: "I haven't experienced this, but it makes me think of…" or "During that time, my life looked like…" Maybe you are not married, or not a parent, and so in response to such questions you might reflect instead on what that experience has been for you.

The key is to pay very close attention to what arises in you in response to the prompt and allow those memories to come forth.

## WHEN MEMORIES FEEL PAINFUL

Some memories may elicit sorrow, regret, longing, or even pain. Move gently. These are aspects of us that very often still need to be heard, held and healed. Healing begins with our own willingness to look kindly at what was. It may be helpful to find a person who you can share your story with first. Name what you can, and let the rest, rest in God's hands.

Remember that even the hardest chapters belong within your story of faith. Through them, God has been quietly shaping compassion, humility, and strength — gifts you may only now be ready to see.

# SOME SUGGESTIONS FOR HOW TO JOURNAL

**Get Familiar** — Look through the journal or at the "Listing of Prompts" section to gain some idea of what you will encounter in the coming pages. Then, when you are ready to write…

**Begin With a Prayer** — Ask God to bring to mind people and moments that shaped your faith.

**Move Freely** — Write in any order. Write at your own pace. Don't force responses. Mark which entries you complete in the "Listing of Prompts" section for ease of reference.

**Trust Yourself** — Some prompts may seem vague. Trust your interpretation.

**Be Honest and Real** — Remember that everything is relevant to God's work in your life—even those times where you didn't know God yet. Include both joy and struggle; the 'good' and the 'bad' of life.

**Tell Your Story** — Add memories, questions and insights that come to mind. Where there is not enough space to answer the prompt, use the extra space provided in the "Stories Continued" section. Cross-reference page numbers so your thoughts remain connected.

**Close in Gratitude** — When you finish writing, read back over your words and give thanks for the opportunity and time to journal and for your life held in grace.

MAY YOU FIND *Joy* in revisiting your *life of* FAITH — & COURAGE in sharing it.

# 01

# ABOUT ME

Every story of faith is
rooted in real life, and is born
in a particular place, time
and person.

Before you share the stories
of how your faith grew and changed
and the meaning its had,
begin with who you are now —
the people and places that shape you,
the life you're living,
and where your faith has
brought you so far.

*Before I formed you*
in the womb
**I KNEW YOU,**
*Before you were born*
I SET YOU
APART.

---

JEREMIAH 1:5

*Insert a baby photo of yourself here*

## FULL NAME

_____

## MEANING OF MY NAME

_____
_____
_____

## DATE OF BIRTH

_____

## PLACE AND TIME OF MY BIRTH

_____
_____

## PARENTS

_____
_____
_____

## SPOUSE / PARTNER

_____

## CHILDREN

## GRANDCHILDREN

## GRANDPARENTS

## PETS

*Insert a current photo
of yourself here*

**PLACE I CURRENTLY LIVE**

_____

_____

**PLACES I HAVE PREVIOUSLY LIVED**

_____

_____

_____

_____

**ROLES AND IDENTITIES ACROSS MY LIFETIME**

_____

_____

_____

_____

_____

_____

_____

_____

_____

_____

ABOUT ME

# A VIEW FROM ABOVE

To take a view from above
is to step back and see your
faith at a distance.

The foundations, pillars, and favorites
that have shaped you come
into focus — the church you
call home, the Scriptures
you return to, the practices
that steady your soul.

This is the landscape of
your life with God.

The SPIRIT of God
*has made me;*
THE BREATH OF
**the Almighty**
*gives me life.*

---

JOB 33:4

**CURRENT DENOMINATION**

_____

**CURRENT CHURCH**

_____

_____

**PREVIOUS DENOMINATION OR CHURCH AFFILIATIONS**

_____

_____

_____

_____

**BAPTISM DATE AND LOCATION**

_____

**OTHER SIGNIFICANT CEREMONIES AND RITES**

_____

_____

_____

_____

_____

## MOSAIC OF FAITH

*Faith is kept alive through and shaped by countless hands and hearts. Record the names of the people in your life who add light, texture, and strength to your faith. They may or may not be people of faith themselves, yet nourish yours.*

**CURRENT PASTOR, MINISTER OR SPIRITUAL GUIDE**

_____

**PREVIOUS PASTORS, MINISTERS OR SPIRITUAL GUIDES**

_____

_____

_____

**BIBLE VERSION OF CHOICE AND WHY**

_____

_____

_____

**CHERISHED OBJECTS OF FAITH**

_____

_____

_____

**MEANINGFUL SYMBOLS OF FAITH**

_____

_____

_____

## EVOLVING FAITH

*Create a timeline of the key moments in your evolving faith.*

**EVOLVING FAITH (CONTINUED)**

## SEASONS OF FAITH IN ONE WORD

*Describe each season of faith in one word.*
*e.g. curiosity, generosity, doubt, suffering, awe...*

0 – 5 years

5 – 8 years

9 – 12 years

13 – 18 years

19 – 25 years

26 – 35 years

36 – 45 years

46 – 55 years

56 – 70 years

71 – 80 years

80 and beyond

## WAYS I EXPRESS MY FAITH

*Note down all the ways you currently or previously have expressed your faith. Some people pray, some preach and teach, others sing, dance and make art.*

IN THE LIVES OF SAINTS
*we learn that* GRACE
is not given to
MAKE US LESS HUMAN,
*but more fully*
ALIVE.

THOMAS MERTON

## MOST INSPIRATIONAL CHRISTIAN FIGURE OR SAINT

## FAVORITE CHRISTIAN AUTHORS AND SPEAKERS

## BOOKS THAT NURTURE MY FAITH

_____

_____

_____

_____

_____

_____

_____

## MOST INFLUENTIAL BOOK

_____

_____

_____

_____

_____

_____

_____

## INSPIRING ART WORK OR IMAGES OF FAITH

---
---
---
---
---

*Insert an image below.*

## SCRIPTURES THAT MARKED MY LIFE

*Identify six scriptures and share how they have shaped your faith.*

**01** ———————————————————
_____
_____
_____
_____

**02** ———————————————————
_____
_____
_____
_____

**03** ———————————————————
_____
_____
_____
_____

## SCRIPTURES THAT MARKED MY LIFE

*Continued.*

**04** ———————————————————————

———————————————————————

———————————————————————

———————————————————————

**05** ———————————————————————

———————————————————————

———————————————————————

———————————————————————

**06** ———————————————————————

———————————————————————

———————————————————————

———————————————————————

**MOST LOVED HYMN OR WORSHIP SONG**

_____

_____

_____

_____

_____

_____

*Write it out in full.*

*There are places where* HEAVEN & EARTH MEET, AND WHEN WE enter them, *we remember* WHO WE ARE.

FREDERICK BUECHNER

## SACRED PLACES

*Mark on the map places that are important to your faith.
They may be places you've visited, but also those you've read about or
studied, or simply inspired you.*

## THE PLACE THAT MOST SUPPORTS MY FAITH

## EXPERIENCE OF PILGRIMAGE

## HOLY-DAYS THAT I OBSERVE

# 03

# BEGINNINGS OF FAITH

Before faith was something
you chose, it was something you
encountered — through family,
community, questions, or quiet
moments of wonder.

Here, look back to where
faith first touched your life and
how early experiences
began to shape what
you believe today.

*He makes*
*EVERYTHING*
*beautiful*
in its TIME.

— ◆ —

ECCLESIASTES 3:11

## BRIEFLY DESCRIBE YOUR CHILDHOOD. WHAT WAS IMPORTANT TO YOU?

## WHAT IS YOUR FIRST MEMORY OF LEARNING ABOUT GOD?

## FAITH FIRSTS

*Recall your first memories and encounters with God.*

**My first memory of attending church…**

_____
_____
_____
_____

**My first memory of prayer…**

_____
_____
_____
_____

**My first memory of hearing a hymn or worship song…**

_____
_____
_____
_____

## FAITH FIRSTS

*Continued...*

**The first pastor, minister or teacher I had…**

_____
_____
_____
_____

**The first Bible or object of faith I was given…**

_____
_____
_____
_____

**The first Bible verse or story I recall hearing…**

_____
_____
_____
_____

## WHAT DID "GOD" MEAN TO YOU AS A CHILD?

## WHAT DID "BEING CHRISTIAN" MEAN TO YOU AS A CHILD?

## DO YOU RECALL A PARTICULAR TIME YOU FELT COMFORTED BY (THE IDEA OF) GOD?

## DO YOU RECALL A PARTICULAR TIME YOU FELT AFRAID (BY THE IDEA) OF GOD?

BUT JESUS SAID,
*Let the children come*
to me,
*and do not hinder them,*
FOR THE KINGDOM OF HEAVEN
belongs TO THEM.

---◆---

MATTHEW 19:14

## WHAT CHILDHOOD EVENT STRENGTHENED YOUR FAITH?

## WHAT CHILDHOOD EVENT LED YOU TO QUESTION YOUR FAITH?

## LINEAGE OF FAITH

*Draw your faith family tree. Who was behind your introduction to God? Trace back their lineage as far as you can.*

## FAITH IN MY FAMILY OF ORIGIN

**How did faith show up in your family? My family…**

- ☐ Attended church
- ☐ Said grace at meal times
- ☐ Prayed before bed
- ☐ Read Bible stories
- ☐ Observed faith-related holidays
- ☐ Listened to faith-related music
- ☐ Tried to live by God's word
- ☐ Displayed objects of faith

**What else?**

**Describe the atmosphere of faith in your home during childhood.**

_____
_____
_____
_____
_____
_____
_____
_____
_____
_____

**A STANDOUT MEMORY OF FAITH IN YOUR FAMILY**

*Insert a photo
of your family of origin here*

**DESCRIBE THE AREA YOU GREW UP IN.
HOW DID IT – OR DIDN'T IT – SHAPE YOUR FAITH?**

## WAS THERE A TIME YOU EXPERIENCED NATURE AS A SIGN OF GOD?

## WHAT OTHER THINGS WERE "SIGNS OF GOD" FOR YOU AS A CHILD?

BEGINNINGS OF FAITH

## EARLY THOUGHTS ON HEAVEN

*What would your child-self have responded to the following:*

I thought you got to heaven by…

I imagined heaven would be filled with…

I thought the people there would be…

I wondered if _____ would be there too.

In heaven I thought you could…

I imagined the color of heaven to be….

I imagined heaven would smell like….

I believed _____ was in heaven.

I thought that getting to heaven would be…

The first thing I'd do when I got to heaven was…

**WHAT DID YOU KNOW OR THINK ABOUT OTHER FAITHS OR RELIGIONS AND THEIR FOLLOWERS?**

**WHAT EARLY EXPERIENCE TAUGIIT YOU THAT CARING FOR OTHERS WAS A WAY OF SHOWING GOD'S LOVE?**

AND BE KIND
*to one another,*
*forgiving*
each other
*just as GOD also in*
CHRIST forgave you.

———◆———

EPHESIANS 4:32

**A TIME SOMEONE MODELLED FORGIVENESS TO YOU AS A CHILD.**

**IF YOU COULD THANK ONE PERSON FOR NURTURING YOUR EARLY FAITH – WHO WOULD IT BE?**

**DO YOU THINK GOD WAS GUIDING YOU TOWARDS A LIFE OF FAITH BEFORE YOU KNEW IT?**

_____

_____

_____

_____

_____

_____

_____

_____

# 04

# GROWING & QUESTIONING

Every seed of faith
must stretch toward the
light. The person who once
prayed in wonder begins
to think, to question,
to search.

These growing years
teach us that faith is not fixed
and unchanging but a living
conversation between
our heart and God.

*Lord,*
# I BELIEVE;
*help my unbelief!*

---

MARK 9:24

**BRIEFLY DESCRIBE YOUR TEENAGE YEARS.
WHAT WAS IMPORTANT TO YOU?**

_____

_____

_____

_____

_____

_____

_____

_____

**WHAT DID YOUR LIFE OF FAITH LOOK LIKE
AT THAT TIME?**

_____

_____

_____

_____

_____

_____

_____

_____

## WHO AROUND YOU LIVED A LIFE OF FAITH?

## WHAT QUESTIONS ABOUT GOD SURFACED DURING THAT TIME?

## CHANGING THROUGH FAITH

*Think of four areas that changed as your faith grew. e.g. values, understanding, attitudes, feelings, sense of purpose, or sense of self.*

**01** ――――――――
___
___
___

**02** ――――――――
___
___
___

**03** ――――――――
___
___
___

**04** ――――――――
___
___
___

**DESCRIBE A MOMENT YOU FELT GOD'S PRESENCE.**

_____
_____
_____
_____
_____
_____
_____
_____

**DESCRIBE A MOMENT YOU FELT DISTANT FROM GOD.**

_____
_____
_____
_____
_____
_____
_____
_____

## TRUST in the Lord

*with all thine heart;* AND LEAN NOT UNTO THINE OWN understanding. *In all thy ways* *acknowledge him,* AND HE SHALL DIRECT THY PATH.

PROVERBS 3:5-6

**HOW DID YOUR FAITH INFORM YOUR SENSE OF SELF?**

**WHEN DID FAITH START TO FEEL LIKE YOU OWN?**

**WHO OR WHAT WAS THE GREATEST SUPPORT TO YOUR GROWING FAITH?**

_____
_____
_____
_____
_____
_____
_____
_____

**WHO OR WHAT WAS THE GREATEST CHALLENGE TO GROWING YOUR FAITH?**

_____
_____
_____
_____
_____
_____
_____
_____

**WHO HELPED YOU THROUGH A TIME OF DOUBT AND CONFUSION?**

_____
_____
_____
_____
_____
_____
_____

**WHAT ROLE DID COMMUNITY FELLOWSHIP PLAY IN YOUR GROWING FAITH?**

_____
_____
_____
_____
_____
_____
_____

**FOR GOD DOES SPEAK**

*— now one way,*

*now another —*

though no one

*perceives it.*

———◆———

JOB 33:14

## HOW DID FAITH INFLUENCE YOUR APPROACH TO RELATIONSHIPS – FRIENDS, FAMILY OR DATING?

## DID YOU ATTEND YOUTH GROUP, CHURCH CHOIR OR CHRISTIAN CAMPS?

**RECALL A TIME THAT A SCRIPTURE "CAME ALIVE" TO YOU.**

---
---
---
---
---
---
---
---

**WHAT PRACTICES (E.G. PRAYER, SONG, WRITING) HELPED YOU FEEL CLOSE TO GOD?**

---
---
---
---
---
---
---
---

**HOW DID YOU IMAGINE YOUR FUTURE IN LIGHT OF FAITH?**

**LOOKING BACK, WHAT DO YOU WISH SOMEONE HAD TOLD YOU ABOUT FAITH AND LIFE?**

# 05

# LOVE & RELATIONSHIPS

Faith that has
been tested begins to
take root in love.

The questions of early
faith give way to the commitments
of relationship — to loving,
forgiving, and belonging.

Here faith is lived
through the people God
places in our company
and care.

And ABOVE all these *put on* LOVE, which binds everything TOGETHER *in perfect* Harmony.

COLOSSIANS 3:14

**IN MY RELATIONSHIPS WITH FAMILY,
LOVE IS EXPRESSED AS...**

_____
_____
_____
_____
_____
_____
_____
_____

**IN MY RELATIONSHIPS WITH FRIENDS,
LOVE IS EXPRESSED AS...**

_____
_____
_____
_____
_____
_____
_____
_____

**MY FAITH INFLUENCED WHO I CHOSE TO LOVE OR HOPED TO MARRY BY…**

_____
_____
_____
_____
_____
_____
_____
_____

**THE PRAYERS I HAVE VOICED FOR MY MARRIAGE OR PARTNERSHIP MOST OFTEN INCLUDE…**

_____
_____
_____
_____
_____
_____
_____
_____

**VALUES OR VIRTUES STRENGTHENED THROUGH MARRIAGE / PARTNERSHIP…**

**A TIME WHEN LOVE OR MARRIAGE TESTED MY FAITH WAS…**

*Insert a photo
of your family here*

TRAIN UP A CHILD
in the way he should go;
*even when he is* OLD
he will NOT
*depart from it.*

———◆———

PROVERBS 22:6

**BECOMING A PARENT DEEPENED MY UNDERSTANDING OF GOD'S LOVE BY...**

_____
_____
_____
_____
_____
_____
_____
_____

**THE PRAYERS I HAVE VOICED FOR MY CHILDREN MOST OFTEN INCLUDE...**

_____
_____
_____
_____
_____
_____
_____
_____

**VALUES OR VIRTUES STRENGTHENED
THROUGH PARENTING...**

_____
_____
_____
_____
_____
_____
_____
_____

**A FAMILY TRADITION OR PRACTICE THAT KEEPS
US CLOSE TO GOD IS...**

_____
_____
_____
_____
_____
_____
_____
_____

**OTHER WAYS FAITH IS EXPRESSED IN OUR FAMILY**

_____

_____

_____

_____

_____

_____

_____

_____

**ONE TIME GOD UNEXPECTEDLY PROVIDED
FOR OUR FAMILY WAS…**

_____

_____

_____

_____

_____

_____

_____

_____

A *new* commandment
I GIVE TO YOU,
*love one another:*
just as I have
LOVED YOU,
YOU ARE ALSO TO
*love one another.*

JOHN 13:34

## WHAT ROLE HAVE FRIENDS HAD IN YOUR LIFE OF FAITH?

_____
_____
_____
_____
_____
_____
_____
_____

## A TIME A FRIEND'S HONESTY, ACCOUNTABILITY, CHALLENGE OR EXAMPLE HELPED REFINE MY FAITH...

_____
_____
_____
_____
_____
_____
_____
_____

## CIRCLE OF PRAYER

*Record the names of friends you pray for regularly and who pray for you.*

*Insert a photo of your
friends or community here*

**ONE OF MY FAVORITE MEMORIES WITH MY FAITH COMMUNITY WAS...**

**I HAVE LEARNED THAT LOVE IN COMMUNITY REQUIRES...**

# 06

# WORK & SERVICE

From the circle of love, faith
extends outward into the world.

In work, service and
calling, what was nurtured
at home finds expression
in action.

To labor faithfully is to
join God in the ongoing work of
creation — shaping life through
diligence, compassion,
and purpose.

**OUR WORK** *can only be a* **CALLING** *if it remains as a* **MISSION** OF **SERVICE** to something beyond our *own* **INTEREST.**

—TIM KELLER

## WHEN DID YOU FIRST SENSE THAT YOUR WORK COULD BE A CALLING, NOT JUST A JOB?

## I HAVE DISCOVERED MY CALLING MOST CLEARLY THROUGH…

**THE PERSON WHO MOST SHAPED MY WORK
ETHIC AS A CHRISTIAN WAS…**

**WHAT DOES "SUCCESS" MEAN TO YOU
IN LIGHT OF YOUR FAITH?**

*For we are*
## GOD'S HANDIWORK,
created in
## CHRIST JESUS
*to do good work*
which GOD prepared in advance
*for us to do.*

---

EPHESIANS 2:10

## SERVING THROUGH MY WORK

*Identify the all the job or service positions you have held over the years. Describe the ways you served others in each of those roles.*

**01** ———————————————

_____

_____

_____

**02** ———————————————

_____

_____

_____

**03** ———————————————

_____

_____

_____

**SERVING THROUGH MY WORK**

*Continued...*

**04**

**05**

**06**

# SERVING THROUGH MY WORK

*Continued...*

**07**

**08**

**09**

**WHICH ROLE OR WORK BROUGHT YOU THE GREATEST SENSE OF PURPOSE OR JOY?**

**DESCRIBE A TIME YOU FAILED OR STRUGGLED AT WORK. HOW DID YOUR FAITH GROW?**

**WHAT TEACHINGS AND PRACTICES HELP YOU KEEP PERSPECTIVE AT WORK?**

**WHAT VERSE, QUOTE OR PIECE OF ADVICE HAS MOST HELPED YOU IN YOUR WORK OR SERVICE?**

**EACH OF YOU**
*should use whatever*

# GIFT

*you have received to serve others,*
AS *faithful stewards*
OF GOD'S GRACE
*in its various forms.*

———◆———

PETER 4:10

**I HAVE FOUND MEANING IN ORDINARY TASKS BY REMEMBERING...**

_____
_____
_____
_____
_____
_____
_____

**WHEN DID YOU LEARN THE IMPORTANCE OF SABBATH AND REST?**

_____
_____
_____
_____
_____
_____
_____
_____

# 07

# THROUGH THE VALLEY

Even in a life rich with
love and purpose,
sorrow finds its way in.

The same God who
blesses our labor and our
families also keeps company
with us in loss, suffering,
hardship and challenge.

In the valley,
faith learns endurance
and gentleness.

*Though I walk through* THE VALLEY OF THE shadow of DEATH, *I will fear no evil:* FOR THOU ART WITH ME.

PSALMS 23:4

## HARDSHIP & SUFFERING HAS TAUGHT ME…

_____
_____
_____
_____
_____
_____
_____
_____

## WHAT HAS FAITH LOOKED LIKE FOR YOU IN YOUR MOST DIFFICULT MOMENTS?

_____
_____
_____
_____
_____
_____
_____
_____

## THE HARDEST CHAPTERS OF MY LIFE

*What have been the most notable times of suffering and hardship?
Give that chapter of life a title and name what was most challenging.*

**01** _____
_____

**02** _____
_____

**03** _____
_____

**04** _____
_____

**05** _____
_____

**06** _____
_____

**07** _____
_____

## TRANSITIONS AFTER HARDSHIP

*How did suffering or hardship in each of those chapters resolve, shift or transform? What are the major factors that brought change? And how did each of those chapters end—if they did?*

**01** _____

**02** _____

**03** _____

**04** _____

**05** _____

**06** _____

**07** _____

**A TIME I FELT MOST ALONE OR UNSURE
OF GOD'S PRESENCE WAS…**

**A TIME I SENSED GOD'S COMFORT OR GUIDANCE
IN THE MIDDLE OF HARDSHIP WAS…**

*Now* if we are children,
then *we are heirs* —
HEIRS OF GOD &
CO-HEIRS WITH CHRIST,
*if indeed we share in*
HIS SUFFERINGS
*in order that we may also*
SHARE
in his *Glory.*

ROMANS 8:17-18

## HOW HAS GRIEF SHAPED YOUR VIEW OF ETERNITY, HEAVEN, OR HOPE?

---
---
---
---
---
---
---
---

## FORGIVENESS ONCE FELT IMPOSSIBLE, UNTIL…

---
---
---
---
---
---
---
---

**GOING THROUGH MY OWN SUFFERING HAS CHANGED HOW I RESPOND TO / ACT TOWARDS...**

**EMOTIONS THAT HAVE BEEN THE MOST DIFFICULT TO EXPERIENCE AND PROCESS ARE...**

*If we have no*
# PEACE,
*it is because*
we have FORGOTTEN
that we
# BELONG
TO EACH OTHER.

———◆———

MOTHER TERESA

## RIVER OF SUPPORT

*Write down the names of particular people, verses, songs, objects, activities that sustained you during times of suffering.*

**A TIME SUFFERING CHANGED THE DIRECTION OF MY LIFE WAS…**

_____
_____
_____
_____
_____
_____
_____
_____

**WHAT WAS ONE DIFFICULT EXPERIENCE THAT OVER TIME REVEALED UNEXPECTED GOOD?**

_____
_____
_____
_____
_____
_____
_____
_____

# 08

# MOUNTAINTOP MOMENTS

Suffering is never the
whole story. From every dark
place, light rises again.

Laughter, healing, small mercies
burst forth, renewing the soul;
joy returns, dancing in the
space where pain once was.

As prayers are answered,
blessings flow abundantly
once again.

# JOY
is the *serious*
# BUSINESS
of *heaven*

---

C.S. LEWIS

**WHAT KIND OF EXPERIENCES WOULD YOU CONSIDER "MOUNTAINTOP MOMENTS"?**

**WITHOUT THESE EXPERIENCES LIFE WOULD BE...**

## THE MOUNTAINTOP CHAPTERS OF MY LIFE

*What have been the chapters of your life that have brought you to the 'mountaintop'. Give them a title and name*

**01** _____
_____

**02** _____
_____

**03** _____
_____

**04** _____
_____

**05** _____
_____

**06** _____
_____

**07** _____
_____

## BLESSINGS FROM THE MOUNTAINTOP

*What impact did these experiences have on you moving forward?
How did you feel? What did you now know? What changed?*

**01** _____
_____

**02** _____
_____

**03** _____
_____

**04** _____
_____

**05** _____
_____

**06** _____
_____

**07** _____
_____

**A TIME WHEN JOY FILLED ME
UNEXPECTEDLY WAS…**

**A MOMENT WHEN I FELT GOD'S PRESENCE
MORE VIVIDLY THAN EVER WAS…**

### ONE PRAYER THAT WAS ANSWERED IN A WAY THAT AMAZED ME WAS…

_____
_____
_____
_____
_____
_____
_____
_____
_____

### I HAVE WITNESSED WHAT I CAN ONLY DESCRIBE AS A MIRACLE WHEN…

_____
_____
_____
_____
_____
_____
_____
_____
_____

I HAVE FOUGHT THE
*GOOD* fight,
*I have finished*
THE RACE,
*I have kept the faith.*
NOW there is in store for me
THE CROWN OF
*righteousness.*

---

2 TIMOTHY 4:7-8

## THE MOST MEANINGFUL RETREAT, CAMP, OR GATHERING I'VE ATTENDED WAS…

## MY IDEA OF HEAVEN ON EARTH IS…

## MOUNTAIN OF BLESSINGS

*Write down the names of particular people, experiences, gifts and talents, and anything else you that you consider a blessing in your life.*

**WHAT HAS EXPERIENCING MOUNTAINTOP MOMENTS TAUGHT YOU ABOUT GOD AND LIFE?**

**WHAT EXPERIENCE STRENGTHENED YOUR TRUST AND FAITH IN GOD?**

*Every* GOOD & PERFECT GIFT *is from above,* COMING DOWN FROM *the father* of lights, *who does not change* LIKE SHIFTING SHADOWS.

---

JAMES 1:17

## A MOUNTAINTOP MOMENT I SHARED WITH ANOTHER WAS...

# EVERYDAY FAITH

The lows of our
sufferings and highs of our
joy arise within the rhythm
of ordinary days.

In the everyday, the glow
of worship becomes a steady
warmth of presence — in dishes
washed, prayers whispered,
kindness given without notice.

Faith finds its home here.

SO WHETHER YOU *eat or drink* or whatever you do *do it all for the* GLORY of God.

1 CORINTHIANS 10:31

## THE SIMPLICITY OF FAITH

The first thing that connects me to God each morning is…

A daily task that has become an act of prayer for me is…

I'm learning that holiness can be found even in …

When I'm busy or distracted, I return to faith by…

Ordinary conversations often become sacred when…

A simple habit that helps me stay close to God each day is...

On quiet afternoons, I like to pause and…

I sense God's peace most in small tasks like…

Caring for my home or garden teaches me about…

When evening comes and I slow down, I thank God for…

My favourite time and way to pray or reflect each day is…

## A DAY OF FAITH

*Identify all the moments, activities, objects, people, and places etc. in your average day that strengthen, remind you, express or reflect God's and your faith.*

**A DAILY CHALLENGE THAT STRENGTHENS
MY FAITH IS…**

_____

_____

_____

_____

_____

_____

_____

_____

**I TRY TO SHOW GOD'S LOVE THROUGH SMALL ACTS
EACH DAY SUCH AS…**

_____

_____

_____

_____

_____

_____

_____

_____

**DOES FAITH SHAPE YOUR PRIORITIES EACH DAY?**

**WHAT FOOD DO YOU ASSOCIATE WITH YOUR FAITH AND WHY?**

**HOW DOES FAITH INFLUENCE YOUR APPROACH TO YOUR PHYSICAL HEALTH DAY-TO-DAY?**

---
---
---
---
---
---
---
---

**HOW DOES FAITH INFLUENCE YOUR APPROACH TO YOUR MENTAL AND EMOTIONAL HEALTH DAY-TO-DAY?**

---
---
---
---
---
---
---
---

*Your word* is a LAMP to my *FEET* and a LIGHT on my *PATH*.

PSALMS 119:105

**WHEN I'M TIRED OR DISCOURAGED, FAITH HELPS ME BY…**

**A PERSON WHOSE FAITH REGULARLY STEADIES MY OWN IS…**

# THE HARVEST

Over time, the small
steps we take to grow,
strengthen and embody our
faith in daily life
becomes wisdom.

What once felt routine
begins to reveal its meaning,
and we see the
deep truths and teachings
God has been speaking
and nurturing in us.

IS NOT
*wisdom*
FOUND AMONG THE AGED?
Does not
LONG LIFE
*bring understanding?*

—◆—

JOB 12:12

## THE FRUITS OF FAITH

*Write below the spiritual fruits your faith has grown, such as peace, forgiveness, trust, love, endurance.*

## GATHERED WISDOM

*Record a lesson, insight or piece of wisdom each of the prompts brings to mind in relation to living a life of faith.*

### Being a child
*(e.g. laughter and play can be holy)*

_____
_____
_____

### Being a teenager
*(e.g. learn to question things without losing hope)*

_____
_____
_____

### First encounters with God
*(e.g. God often speaks first through love, not words)*

_____
_____
_____

### Parenting

_____
_____
_____

# GATHERED WISDOM

*Continued...*

### Friends

_____
_____
_____

### Community

_____
_____
_____

### Prayer

_____
_____
_____

### Gratitude

_____
_____
_____

# GATHERED WISDOM

*Continued...*

### Patience

___
___
___

### Joy

___
___
___

### Courage

___
___
___

### Forgiveness

___
___
___

The FEAR
*of the Lord*
IS THE BEGINNING OF
WISDOM

PSALM 111:10

# GATHERED WISDOM

*Continued...*

**Grief and Loss**

---

**Doubt**

---

**Anger**

---

**Fear**

---

# GATHERED WISDOM

*Continued...*

### Calling

_____
_____
_____

### Change

_____
_____
_____

### Growth

_____
_____
_____

### Grace

_____
_____
_____

## OVER THE YEARS, MY UNDERSTANDING OF GOD HAS CHANGED IN THAT…

_____
_____
_____
_____
_____
_____
_____
_____

## I USED TO THINK FAITH MEANT… BUT NOW I BELIEVE IT MEANS…

_____
_____
_____
_____
_____
_____
_____
_____

**AN EXPERIENCE THAT COMPLETELY RESHAPED MY FAITH WAS…**

_____

_____

_____

_____

_____

_____

_____

**ONE LESSON GOD HAS TAUGHT ME AGAIN AND AGAIN IS…**

_____

_____

_____

_____

_____

_____

_____

_____

DO NOT *conform*
to the pattern of the
WORLD,
but be
*transformed*
BY THE REVIEWING OF
*your* MIND.

—•◆•—

ROMANS 12:2

**A QUESTION OF FAITH I ONCE FEARED ASKING
BUT NOW WELCOME IS…**

_____

_____

_____

_____

_____

_____

_____

**THE LONGER I'VE LIVED A LIFE OF FAITH,
THE MORE I UNDERSTAND THAT…**

_____

_____

_____

_____

_____

_____

_____

### I UNDERSTAND "LOVE YOUR ENEMIES" TO MEAN…

### TODAY, WHEN I ENCOUNTER PEOPLE WITH BELIEFS THAT DIFFER FROM MINE I…

LOVE your *enemies,* DO GOOD TO THOSE *who* HATE you, *BLESS* those who *CURSE you,* PRAY *FOR THOSE* mistreat you.

---

LUKE 6:27-28

**WHAT I'VE LEARNED ABOUT WALKING WITH
GOD IN ORDINARY LIFE IS...**

_____

_____

_____

_____

_____

_____

_____

**THE CLEAREST SIGN OF SPIRITUAL MATURITY
TO ME IS...**

_____

_____

_____

_____

_____

_____

_____

_____

# THE HEART OF THANKS

Wisdom ripens into gratitude.

As we look back, the threads of grace begin to show — the answered prayers, the unexpected gifts, even what we thought were delays and detours.

Gratitude grows when we realize that none of it was wasted — that all moments, people and mercies have shaped who we've become.

I WILL REMEMBER
*the deeds of the Lord*
# YES,
I will remember
*YOUR wonders of*
# ALL.

—◆—

PSALMS 77:11

**GIVING THANKS TO GOD TO ME MEANS...**

_____
_____
_____
_____
_____
_____
_____
_____

**MY FIRST EXPERIENCE OF GIVING THANKS WAS...**

_____
_____
_____
_____
_____
_____
_____
_____
_____

**WHEN SOMEONE HAS EXPRESSED GRATITUDE TO ME, I FELT…**

_____
_____
_____
_____
_____
_____
_____
_____

**A MOMENT WHEN I REALIZED HOW MUCH I HAVE RECEIVED WAS…**

_____
_____
_____
_____
_____
_____
_____
_____

**A TIME I WITNESSED THE POWER OF GRATITUDE WAS...**

_____
_____
_____
_____
_____
_____
_____
_____

**A TIME GRATITUDE TRANSFORMED MY OUTLOOK WAS...**

_____
_____
_____
_____
_____
_____
_____
_____

> *Give thanks* to the LORD FOR HE IS GOOD; his love endures *forever.*

1 CHRONICLES 16:34

**A DIFFICULT EXPERIENCE THAT DEEPENED MY GRATITUDE WAS…**

**THE HABITS OF FAITH THAT HAVE HELPED ME STAY THANKFUL ARE…**

## GRATITUDE ACROSS TIME

*We can be grateful in the moment, in hindsight and enduringly over the years.
Identify those things you are grateful for and how you expressed your gratitude.*

**Things I have felt enduringly grateful for over the years...**

_____
_____
_____
_____
_____
_____
_____
_____
_____
_____
_____
_____
_____
_____
_____
_____
_____

**Things I was grateful for in hindsight…**

**Things I felt immediately grateful for…**

GRATITUDE unlocks the *fullness* of LIFE...

MELODY BEATTIE

**WHEN I LOOK BACK OVER MY LIFE, I SEE GOD'S HAND MOST CLEARLY IN…**

---

**WHEN DID YOU UNDERSTAND THE IMPORTANCE OF GIVING THANKS IN LEADING A LIFE OF FAITH?**

## SHARE A PRAYER OF GRATITUDE

# THE OFFERING

Gratitude stirs a longing
to bless others with what life
has taught us — planting seeds
of hope and inspiration in
those who follow us.

What we've received in grace,
we now give in love.

Our words and witness
become a living offering, passed
from one generation to the next,
testifying that God's
goodness endures.

WE WILL TELL
the next generation
*the praiseworthy*
DEEDS of the
*LORD.*

PSALM 78:4

**WHOSE LEGACY OR TESTIMONY HAS INSPIRED YOUR LIFE OF FAITH?**

_____

_____

_____

_____

_____

_____

_____

_____

**WHY ARE LEGACY AND TESTIMONY IMPORTANT?**

_____

_____

_____

_____

_____

_____

_____

_____

## WHAT HAVE YOU CARRIED FORWARD FROM YOUR FAMILY OR MENTORS IN FAITH?

## ONE MESSAGE I WOULD SHARE WITH MY YOUNGER SELF IS...

## TO MY FAMILY

*Write a verse from scripture or worship song you would like to dedicate to your family.*

*Insert a photo
of your family here*

## TO MY FAMILY

**I thank God for our family because…**

_____

_____

**I hope you will always remember that…**

_____

_____

**I pray our family will be known for…**

_____

_____

**I have learned through our story that…**

_____

_____

**I give thanks for the ways we have…**

_____

_____

## TO MY FAMILY

**I hope you will carry forward...**

_____

_____

**I want you to know that even when life changes...**

_____

_____

**I hope you will tell the stories of our family that...**

_____

_____

**If my life teaches you anything, let it be that...**

_____

_____

**I want you to remember that our family's truest story is one of...**

_____

_____

## TO MY FAMILY

*Record personal notes to individuals, such as verses from scripture, quotes, statements from the heart.*

## TO MY FAMILY

*Continued.*

## TO MY FAMILY

*Continued.*

*Friendship* IS THE INSTRUMENT by which GOD reveals *to each of us* THE BEAUTIES *of others.*

C.S. LEWIS

## TO MY FRIENDS

**I thank God for the friendships I've had because...**

_____

_____

**I have learned through friendship that...**

_____

_____

**I pray that the friendships I've had, have shown my friends that...**

_____

_____

**I am grateful for the way my friends have...**

_____

_____

**I hope my friends will always know that...**

_____

_____

## TO MY FRIENDS

*Record personal notes to individual friends. This could be verses from scripture, quotes, statements from the heart.*

## TO MY FRIENDS

*Continued.*

IN TRUE COMMUNITY
*we find safety to be*
**OURSELVES**
and the COURAGE
TO BECOME MORE FULLY
*who God made us*
to be.

—◆—

PALKER J. PALMER

## TO MY COMMUNITY

**I thank my community for teaching me that…**

_____

_____

**I have seen God at work among us when…**

_____

_____

**I pray our community will continue to be known for…**

_____

_____

**I am grateful for the way my friends have…**

_____

_____

**I hope my part in this community has shown…**

_____

_____

FOR GOD SO
# LOVED
*the world...*

———◆———

JOHN 3:16

## TO THE WORLD

**I pray my life will be remembered as…**

_____

_____

**I believe that God's love can transform…**

_____

_____

**I hope the generations to come will continue to…**

_____

_____

**I want to offer the world this simple truth…**

_____

_____

**I trust that God will use my story to…**

_____

_____

## WHAT DO I MOST HOPE MY LIFE HAS SHOWN ABOUT GOD'S LOVE AND FAITHFULNESS?

# EVERLASTING FAITH

Faith, when lived fully,
does not end but instead deepens.

Even as our bodies grow older,
the heart of trust grows stronger.

The movement of time calls
for reflecting on how faith
continues to unfold, how to find
peace with mortality, and how love
and grace endure beyond
a single lifetime.

If we LIVE
*we live for the Lord;*
And if we *die,*
WE DIE FOR THE LORD.
*So whether we live of die,*
we BELONG
TO THE LORD.

---

ROMANS 14:8

**WHEN I THINK OF ETERNITY, I IMAGINE...**

_____

_____

_____

_____

_____

_____

_____

_____

**THE EXPERIENCE I HAVE WHEN I THINK ABOUT GOD'S FOREVER FAITHFULNESS IS...**

_____

_____

_____

_____

_____

_____

_____

_____

**LOOKING BACK, I SEE THAT MY FAITH HAS ENDURED THROUGH…**

_____
_____
_____
_____
_____
_____
_____
_____

**AT THIS STAGE IN MY LIFE, FAITH IS…**

_____
_____
_____
_____
_____
_____
_____
_____

Jesus said,
'*I am the ressurection
and the* LIFE.
THE ONE WHO
*believes*
in me will LIVE,
*even though they die;*
and whoever lives by
*believing in me*
WILL NEVER DIE.'

———◆———

JOHN 11:25-26

EVERLASTING FAITH

**OVER THE COURSE OF MY LIFE, THE IDEA OF DEATH HAS…**

_____
_____
_____
_____
_____
_____
_____
_____

**MY FAITH HAS SHAPED HOW I THINK ABOUT DEATH BY…**

_____
_____
_____
_____
_____
_____
_____
_____

**THE THOUGHT OF WORLDLY DEATH INFLUENCES HOW I...**

**I IMAGINE MEETING GOD FACE TO FACE AS...**

## IN MY FINAL WORLDLY MOMENTS

**Others should celebrate my life with the following verses, hymns, worship songs and prayers…**

_____
_____
_____
_____

**I wish to be surrounded by…**

_____
_____
_____
_____

**I wish to hear, smell and feel…**

_____
_____
_____
_____

**I wish others to remember that…**

_____
_____
_____

## TODAY'S THOUGHTS ON HEAVEN

*You reflected on how you, as a child, thought of heaven (on page 46), What are your thoughts today?*

I think you get to heaven by…

I imagine heaven will be filled with…

I think the people there will be…

I wonder if _____ will be there too.

In heaven I think you can…

I imagine the color of heaven to be….

I imagine heaven will smell like….

I believe _____ is in heaven.

I think that getting to heaven will be…

The first thing I'll do when I get to heaven is…

*And the Lord answered me,*
and said,
WRITE THE VISION,
and *make it plain,*
so that the one
*who reads it*
MAY RUN.

—◆—

HABAKKUK 2:2

**I DRAW STRENGTH FOR EACH NEW DAY FROM...**

**THINGS I AM STILL LEARNING AND WAYS THAT GOD IS STILL SHAPING ME...**

## THE WAYS I STILL FEEL CALLED TO CONTRIBUTE OR HELP OTHERS INCLUDE…

## I WANT MY FINAL CHAPTER OF LIFE TO REFLECT GOD'S LOVE BY…

*Insert a photo or image representing
how you wish to be remembered.*

# A CLOSING BLESSING

A blessing invokes God's favor,
grace, or protection over a person,
situation, or thing.

It expresses both
gratitude and divine generosity,
recognizing that all goodness
comes from God
and that humans are invited
to share in that abundance by
speaking or receiving words of
life, peace, and hope.

### *A Closing Blessing to You*

May the Lord bless you and keep you.
May His face shine upon you and give you peace.
May your roots grow deep in His love,
and your life bear witness to His grace.

May every joy remind you of His goodness,
and every sorrow draw you nearer to His heart.
May the work He began in you
be brought to completion until the day you
stand before Him in glory.

And may your faith
— lived, tested, and renewed —
shine as a light for those who walk the
road after you.

## *Your Final Word*

*As a final entry to this legacy journal,
write your own blessing using the following pages.*

*It may be a final prayer, a word of hope,
or a wish for those who will follow in your footsteps.
Or all those things and more.*

*Let it carry the heart of your faith and the
love you have known through God.*

A CLOSING BLESSING

# STORIES CONTINUED

STORIES CONTINUED

STORIES CONTINUED

# LISTING OF PROMPTS

*Below is a list of the topic/theme explored in each prompt —
visit the page to find the full prompt.*

## 01 ABOUT ME     1

- ☐ My full name     4
- ☐ The symbolism or meaning of my name     4
- ☐ My date of birth     4
- ☐ The place and time of my birth     4
- ☐ My parents     4
- ☐ My spouse or partner     4
- ☐ My children     5
- ☐ My grandchildren     5
- ☐ My grandparents     5
- ☐ My pets     5
- ☐ The place I currently live     7
- ☐ Places I have previously lived     7
- ☐ Roles and identities I hold or have held     7

## 02 A VIEW FROM ABOVE     11

- ☐ My current denomination     13
- ☐ My current church     13
- ☐ My previous denomination or church affiliations     13
- ☐ My baptism date and location     13
- ☐ Other significant ceremonies and rites     13
- ☐ The mosaic of my faith     14
- ☐ My current pastor, minister, or spiritual guide     15
- ☐ My previous pastors, ministers, or spiritual guides     15
- ☐ My preferred Bible version     15
- ☐ My cherished objects of faith     15
- ☐ My meaningful symbols of faith     15

| | | |
|---|---|---|
| ☐ | How my faith has evolved | 16 |
| ☐ | My seasons of faith in one word | 18 |
| ☐ | Ways I express my faith | 19 |
| ☐ | Inspirational Christian figures or saints | 21 |
| ☐ | Favorite Christian authors, thinkers, and speakers | 21 |
| ☐ | Favorite books that nurture my faith | 22 |
| ☐ | Inspirational artwork or images | 23 |
| ☐ | Scriptures that have impacted me | 24 |
| ☐ | Favorite hymn or worship song | 26 |
| ☐ | Sacred places in my life | 28 |
| ☐ | Supportive places that nurture my faith | 29 |
| ☐ | My experiences of pilgrimage | 29 |
| ☐ | Holy-days that I observe | 30 |

## 03 BEGINNINGS OF FAITH 33

| | | |
|---|---|---|
| ☐ | My life during childhood | 35 |
| ☐ | My first memory of learning about God | 35 |
| ☐ | My early faith experiences; "faith firsts" | 36 |
| ☐ | What God meant to me as a child | 38 |
| ☐ | What being Christian meant to me as a child | 38 |
| ☐ | A time I felt comforted by the idea of God | 39 |
| ☐ | A time I felt afraid of the idea of God | 39 |
| ☐ | A childhood event that strengthened my faith | 41 |
| ☐ | A childhood event that made me question my faith | 41 |
| ☐ | My lineage of faith | 42 |
| ☐ | My family of origin and faith | 43 |
| ☐ | My standout family memories of faith | 44 |
| ☐ | How my hometown or surroundings shaped my faith | 46 |
| ☐ | Experiencing God in nature | 47 |

| | | |
|---|---|---|
| ☐ | Signs of God I noticed as a child | 47 |
| ☐ | My early thoughts on Heaven | 48 |
| ☐ | My family's thoughts about people of other faiths or beliefs | 49 |
| ☐ | Who modelled caring for others in my early years | 49 |
| ☐ | Who modelled forgiveness for me | 51 |
| ☐ | A person who nurtured my early faith | 51 |
| ☐ | Reflecting on God's presence in my early life | 52 |

## 04 GROWING & QUESTIONING        55

| | | |
|---|---|---|
| ☐ | What was important during my teenage years | 57 |
| ☐ | My life of faith during that time | 57 |
| ☐ | People around me who lived a life of faith | 58 |
| ☐ | Questions about God that surfaced | 58 |
| ☐ | My changing understanding and beliefs | 59 |
| ☐ | Moments I felt God's presence | 60 |
| ☐ | Times I felt distant from God | 60 |
| ☐ | How my faith shaped my sense of self | 62 |
| ☐ | When my faith began to feel like my own | 62 |
| ☐ | My greatest support in faith | 63 |
| ☐ | My greatest challenge in faith | 63 |
| ☐ | People who helped me through doubt and confusion | 64 |
| ☐ | The role of community and fellowship in my faith | 64 |
| ☐ | How faith influenced my relationships | 66 |
| ☐ | My involvement in youth group, church choir, or camps | 66 |
| ☐ | Scripture that became a breakthrough for me | 67 |
| ☐ | Practices that helped me feel close to God | 67 |
| ☐ | How I imagined my future in light of faith | 68 |
| ☐ | What I wish someone had told me about faith and life | 68 |

## 05 LOVE & RELATIONSHIPS — 71

- [ ] How love is expressed in my family relationships — 73
- [ ] How love is expressed in my friendships — 73
- [ ] How my faith has influenced who I chose to love — 74
- [ ] Prayers I have voiced for my marriage or partnership — 74
- [ ] Values or virtues strengthened through partnership — 75
- [ ] Times when love or marriage tested my faith — 75
- [ ] How becoming a parent deepened my understanding of love and faith — 78
- [ ] Prayers I have voiced for my children — 78
- [ ] Values or virtues strengthened through parenting — 79
- [ ] Family traditions or practices that keep us close to God — 79
- [ ] Other ways faith is expressed in our family — 80
- [ ] Times God unexpectedly provided for our family — 80
- [ ] The role of friends in my life of faith — 82
- [ ] How a friend's honesty, accountability, challenge, or example shaped me — 82
- [ ] My circle of prayer — 83
- [ ] Favorite memories with my faith community — 85
- [ ] What I have learned about love in community — 85

## 06 WORK & SERVICE — 89

- [ ] When I first sensed my work could be a calling — 91
- [ ] How I have discovered my calling most clearly — 91
- [ ] What success means to me in light of my faith — 92
- [ ] The person who most shaped my work ethic — 92
- [ ] Serving through my work — 94
- [ ] Work that brought me the greatest sense of purpose — 97
- [ ] Times I failed or struggled at work — 97
- [ ] Teachings and practices that help me keep perspective at work — 98

| ☐ | Supportive verses, quotes, advice, or encouragement that guide my work | 98 |
| ☐ | Finding meaning in ordinary tasks | 100 |
| ☐ | How I learned the importance of Sabbath and rest | 100 |

## 07 THROUGH THE VALLEY — 103

| ☐ | What hardship and suffering has taught me | 105 |
| ☐ | What faith has looked like in my most difficult moments | 105 |
| ☐ | The hardest chapters of my life | 106 |
| ☐ | Transitions I faced after hardship | 107 |
| ☐ | Times I felt most alone or unsure of God's presence | 108 |
| ☐ | God's comfort or guidance in the midst of hardship | 108 |
| ☐ | How grief has shaped my view of eternity, Heaven, and hope | 110 |
| ☐ | When forgiveness once felt impossible | 110 |
| ☐ | How suffering has impacted the way I respond to others | 111 |
| ☐ | My faith and working with emotions | 111 |
| ☐ | The river of support that sustains me | 113 |
| ☐ | Times when suffering changed the direction of my life | 114 |
| ☐ | Out of pain came new understanding or purpose | 114 |

## 08 MOUNTAINTOP MOMENTS — 117

| ☐ | What mountaintop moments mean to me | 119 |
| ☐ | How my life would feel without these experiences | 119 |
| ☐ | The mountaintop chapters of my life | 120 |
| ☐ | Blessings from my mountaintop experiences | 121 |
| ☐ | Times when joy filled me unexpectedly | 122 |
| ☐ | Moments when I felt God's presence vividly | 122 |
| ☐ | Prayers that were answered | 123 |
| ☐ | Witnessing a miracle | 123 |

| | | |
|---|---|---|
| ☐ | Meaningful retreats, camps, or gatherings I have attended | 125 |
| ☐ | My idea of Heaven on earth | 125 |
| ☐ | My mountain of blessings | 126 |
| ☐ | What mountaintop moments have taught me about God and Life | 127 |
| ☐ | Experiences that strengthened my trust and faith in God | 127 |
| ☐ | Shared mountaintop moments | 129 |

## 09 EVERDAY FAITH — 133

| | | |
|---|---|---|
| ☐ | The simplicity of my faith | 135 |
| ☐ | Faith across my day | 136 |
| ☐ | Daily challenges that strengthen my faith | 137 |
| ☐ | How I show God's love through small acts | 137 |
| ☐ | How faith shapes my daily priorities | 138 |
| ☐ | Food and drink I associate with faith | 138 |
| ☐ | Faith's influence on my physical health | 139 |
| ☐ | Faith's influence on my mental and emotional health | 139 |
| ☐ | How faith helps me when I'm tired or discouraged | 141 |
| ☐ | People whose faith steadies my own | 141 |

## 10 THE HARVEST — 144

| | | |
|---|---|---|
| ☐ | The fruits of my faith | 147 |
| ☐ | My gathered wisdom | 148 |
| ☐ | How my understanding of God has changed over the years | 154 |
| ☐ | What I once thought faith meant and what I now believe | 154 |
| ☐ | Experiences that reshaped my faith completely | 155 |
| ☐ | Lessons God has taught me again and again | 155 |
| ☐ | Questions of faith I once feared | 157 |
| ☐ | What I have come to understand through living a life of faith | 157 |

| | | |
|---|---|---|
| ☐ | What "love your enemies" means to me now | 158 |
| ☐ | How I respond to people with beliefs that differ from mine | 158 |
| ☐ | Walking with God in ordinary life | 160 |
| ☐ | What spiritual maturity looks like to me | 160 |

## 11 THE HEART OF THANKS — 163

| | | |
|---|---|---|
| ☐ | What giving thanks to God means to me | 165 |
| ☐ | My first experience of giving thanks | 165 |
| ☐ | How I felt when someone expressed gratitude to me | 166 |
| ☐ | Moments when I realized how much I have received | 166 |
| ☐ | Times I witnessed the power of gratitude | 167 |
| ☐ | How gratitude has transformed my outlook | 167 |
| ☐ | Difficult experiences that deepened my gratitude | 169 |
| ☐ | Habits of faith that help me stay thankful | 169 |
| ☐ | Gratitude across time | 170 |
| ☐ | Seeing God's hand when I look back over my life | 173 |
| ☐ | Understanding the importance of giving thanks | 173 |
| ☐ | My prayer of gratitude | 174 |

## 12 THE OFFERING — 177

| | | |
|---|---|---|
| ☐ | Another's legacy or testimony that has inspired me | 179 |
| ☐ | Why legacy and testimony are important to me | 179 |
| ☐ | What I have carried forward from others | 180 |
| ☐ | A message I would share with my younger self | 180 |
| ☐ | My message to my family | 181 |
| ☐ | My message to my friends | 189 |
| ☐ | My message to my community | 193 |
| ☐ | My message to the world | 195 |
| ☐ | What my life reveals about God's love and faithfulness | 196 |

## 13 EVERLASTING FAITH — 199

- [ ] What I imagine when I think of eternity — 201
- [ ] My thoughts about God's forever faithfulness — 201
- [ ] How my faith has endured through the years — 202
- [ ] What faith means to me at this stage of life — 202
- [ ] How my understanding of death has changed over my life — 204
- [ ] How my faith has shaped the way I think about death — 204
- [ ] How the thought of worldly death influences me — 205
- [ ] How I imagine meeting God face to face — 205
- [ ] What I wish for my final worldly moments — 206
- [ ] My thoughts on Heaven today — 207
- [ ] Where I draw strength for each new day — 208
- [ ] What I am still learning and ways God is still shaping me — 208
- [ ] Ways I still feel called to contribute or help others — 209
- [ ] How I want the final chapter of my life to reflect God's love — 209

## A CLOSING BLESSING — 215

- [ ] My Final Blessing — 218

## DEDICATED PHOTO PAGES

- [ ] Me as a baby/child — 3
- [ ] Me today — 6
- [ ] My family of origin — 45
- [ ] My current family — 76
- [ ] My friends/community — 84
- [ ] My current family — 182
- [ ] How I wish to be remembered — 211

A Life of Faith: The Legacy of God's Work Across My Lifetime

Published by Monkey Magic Press
Copyright © 2025 Cait Buchanan

All rights reserved. No part of this publication may be reproduced in any form or by any means electronic or mechanical, including photocopying, recording, or by any information storage and retrieval system without prior permission in writing from the published. Enquiries should be made to the publisher.

ISBN: 978-1-923639-02-7 (Downriver Edition, paperback)
ISBN: 978-1-923639-03-4 (Downriver Edition, hardback)
ISBN: 978-1-923639-04-1 (Thistle Edition, paperback)
ISBN: 978-1-923639-05-8 (Thistle Edition, hardback)
ISBN: 978-1-923639-06-5 (Stratos Edition, paperback)
ISBN: 978-1-923639-07-2 (Stratos Edition, hardback)

www.ingramcontent.com/pod-product-compliance
Lightning Source LLC
Chambersburg PA
CBHW042045280426
43661CB00094B/1037